FUN WITH SCIENCE

WEATHER

STEVE PARKER

Contents

Use the symbols below to help you identify the three kinds of practical activities in this book.

EXPERIMENTS   **TRICKS**   **THINGS TO MAKE**

Illustrated by Kuo Kang Chen · Peter Bull

Kingfisher Books

Introduction

The first part of this book tells you about the features of our ever-changing weather, such as temperature, winds, clouds, and storms. The middle part shows how weather is measured, and how weather forecasts are made. The last part looks at how the weather affects us—and how we might be affecting the weather.

Throughout the book, there are simple and safe experiments, projects and tricks which you can carry out. The questions on these two pages are based on the scientific ideas explained in this book. As you carry out the experiments, you should be able to answer these questions, and understand more about the weather and how it affects the world around us.

This book covers six main topics:

• Atmosphere, air, temperature, and wind
• Days and seasons, winds, and water currents around the globe
• Moisture in the air, humidity, clouds, rain, snow, and hail
• Thunder and lightning, rainbows, and mirages
• Weather forecasts and weather maps
• How the weather shapes the land and affects animals, plants, and people

A blue line (like the one around the edge of these two pages) indicates the start of a new topic.

▲ How far away is a thunderstorm? (pages 24–25)

▼ What are 'all the colours of the rainbow', and how can you make them for yourself? (page 26)

▼ How does the weather help us to design our homes and buildings? (page 35)

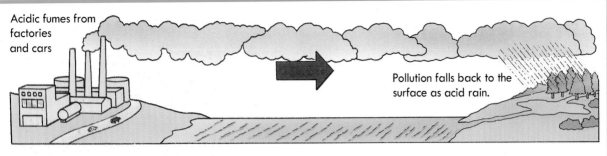

Acidic fumes from factories and cars

Pollution falls back to the surface as acid rain.

▲ Are we changing the weather? How will this affect our world? (pages 38–39)

▲ How do experts predict the weather? And how often are they right? (pages 28–31)

▶ What is wind, and how do we measure it? (pages 10–15)

▼ What is temperature? How can we tell how hot or cold it is? (pages 6–9)

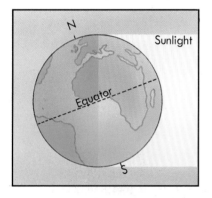

◀ How does the Earth's place in space make day and night? (page 8)

▼ Where does rain come from, and how can you tell the amount that falls? (pages 16–21)

▶ How does the climate affect where plants and animals live? (pages 34–37)

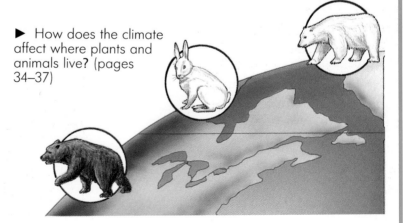

3

An Ocean of Air

It is all around us, but cannot be seen. We can only feel it when it blows on our faces. We can only hear it as it rustles the trees and whistles past buildings. Yet we need to breathe it, or we will die. It is air. Our world is covered with air, called the **atmosphere**. The Earth's gravity keeps it near its surface. Otherwise our spinning planet would fling it off into space.

The Atmosphere

The air in our atmosphere is made of a mixture of colourless gases. These are mainly nitrogen (almost four-fifths), oxygen (one-fifth), plus many other gases, such as argon and carbon dioxide, in tiny amounts.

The air in the atmosphere is densest, or 'thickest', near the ground. As we travel higher it becomes thinner, or more rarefied.

You can feel the weight of air by spreading a large sheet of newspaper flat on a table, and sliding a ruler under one side, as shown below. Hit the ruler hard. It is difficult to lift the paper, because of the weight of air pressing on it. This is called air pressure, and it pushes down at about 1 kilogram per square centimetre.

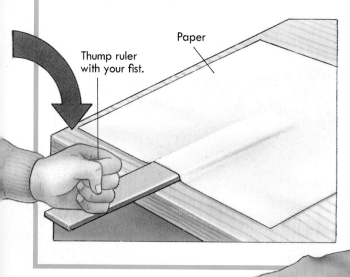

Paper

Thump ruler with your fist.

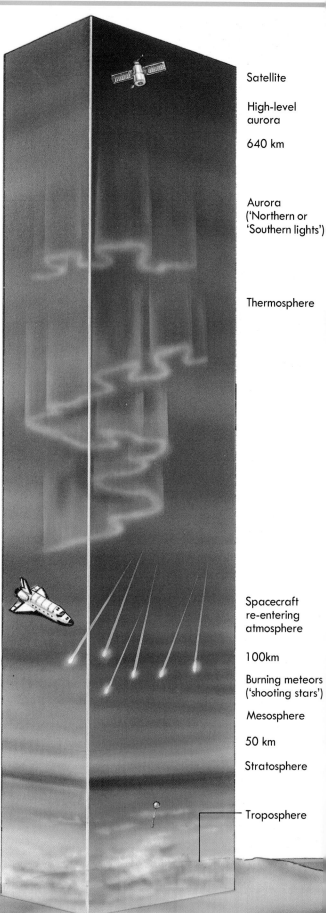

Satellite

High-level aurora

640 km

Aurora ('Northern or 'Southern lights')

Thermosphere

Spacecraft re-entering atmosphere

100km

Burning meteors ('shooting stars')

Mesosphere

50 km

Stratosphere

Troposphere

Using Air to Hold up Water

Air presses in all directions as this trick shows. Fill a clean beaker to the brim with water. Press a square piece of strong card on top to make a good seal. Keeping the beaker over the sink, very carefully turn it over . . . and the water should stay inside!

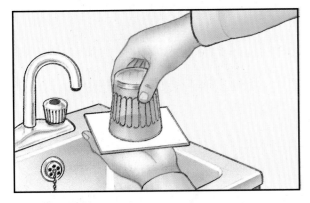

Air pushes upwards on card and keeps water in.

How it works: Air is pressing upwards on the card with enough force to hold the water in place. Push down gently on the corner of the card to break the seal, and air bubbles in it. It now presses downwards as well as up. The card falls away, and the water pours out.

Balancing Balloons!

Air, like most substances, becomes bigger (**expands**) as it is heated. Show that a certain volume of hot air weighs less than the same volume of cold air, by a 'balloon balance'. Blow up two balloons to the same size. Tie each balloon to one end of a long, thin piece of wood (such as a dowel or garden cane). Balance this on a pencil supported by cans or books, and mark the balance point on the wood.

Tip: The balloons are the same size when they touch the saucepan's side.

Saucepan   Balloon

Next, put one balloon in a cold place such as the fridge, and the other in a warm place like the airing cupboard. Let some air out of the warm balloon and blow some air into the cold balloon, so that they are the same size. Now do they balance?

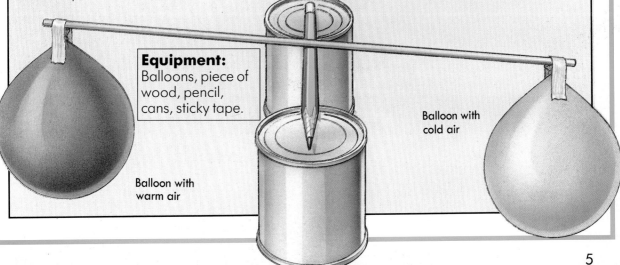

Equipment:
Balloons, piece of wood, pencil, cans, sticky tape.

Balloon with warm air

Balloon with cold air

Testing the Temperature

Air temperature is the 'hotness' or 'coldness' of the air. This is measured by an instrument known as a thermometer.

A scale on the thermometer shows the temperature, which is usually measured in degrees Celsius, written °C. Weather experts use different types of thermometers for different jobs.

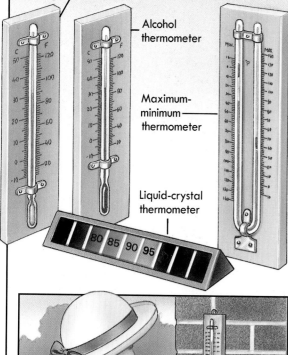

Mercury thermometer

Alcohol thermometer

Maximum-minimum thermometer

Liquid-crystal thermometer

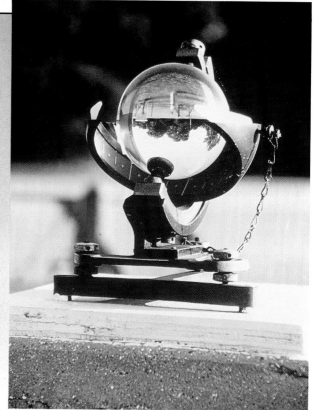

▲ A Campbell-Stokes sunshine recorder. The Sun's rays burn a line on a paper chart. Its length shows hours of sunlight.

◄ An alcohol thermometer is used in very cold places, as the usual mercury freezes at minus 39°C.

In the summer
You can record air temperatures with a thermometer on a shady wall, out of direct sunlight. The temperature on a hot summer day is 25–30°C.

In the winter
In winter the average temperatures are much lower. Water freezes at 0°C. When the air temperature falls below this for a time, ponds and lakes ice over.

Heat from the Sun

The Sun gives out rays of various types. We can see one type – these are light rays, or sunlight. The Sun also gives out heat, in the form of infra-red rays.

How it works: Smooth, shiny surfaces reflect both light and heat rays. Dull, roughened surfaces absorb them.

A simple experiment reveals the power of the Sun to warm different substances by different amounts.

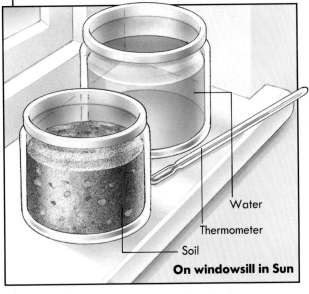

Water

Thermometer

Soil

On windowsill in Sun

▲ In hot places, people wear loose, light coloured clothes. The light colour reflects the Sun's heat, keeping the person cool.

> **Equipment:** Identical glass jars, soil, thermometer, water.

You need two identical glass jars. Carefully half-fill one with dark, fairly dry soil and the other with water. Put them on a sunny window ledge (*above left*), and measure their temperatures straight away with a standard mercury thermometer. (Take extra care, mercury is poisonous.)

Measure their temperatures again after half an hour and one hour. The dark soil absorbs the Sun's heat more quickly than the 'shiny' water and so warms up more rapidly. Now place both jars in a shady place indoors, under a dark cloth (*below left*). Which one cools down more quickly?

Thermometer

Water **Out of Sun**

Soil

Black cloth

Where's Warmest and Coldest

The world's hottest place is Dallol, Ethiopia. Average temperatures over several years were 34.4°C (94°F). Coldest is on Antarctica, where the average temperatures are minus 55°C (minus 70°F)!

Days and Seasons

Planet Earth's movements in space produce the regular changes of day and night, and summer and winter. The planets circle a star, which we call the Sun. It takes one year for the Earth to make a complete circuit. The Earth also spins around itself, once each day.

Summer and Winter, Day and Night

The Earth is not at right angles to the Sun. It is tilted slightly. On its yearly journey around the Sun, the upper part of the Earth (the North) is nearer to the Sun for a few months. The Sun's rays pass almost straight down through the atmosphere, so less of their energy is lost in the atmosphere, and more reaches the surface. It is summer in the North.

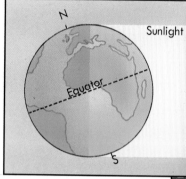

▲ Winter in the North. The Earth's North Pole is tilted away from the Sun.

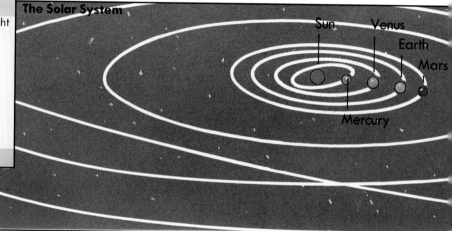

The Solar System

Sun
Venus
Earth
Mars
Mercury

Make a Garden Sundial

You can use the Sun to tell the time, by making a sundial, as shown on the right. Cover a board or large book with white paper for a base. Make a right-angled triangle of card about 20 by 15 by 15 centimetres (8 by 6 by 6 inches), with a flap at the bottom. Stick the flap on the base, using cotton guy ropes if necessary to keep it upright. Draw two curved lines from the corners of the base to the triangle's high side.

Place the sundial where it will get the Sun for most of the day. Use a compass to make the tall vertical side of the triangle points North. Through the day, as the Sun moves it casts a shadow from the card. With a watch to tell the time, mark and label the shadow's position each hour, where it crosses the curved lines. Next day, you can use the sundial to tell the time – provided it is sunny!

Equipment: Compass, card, heavy base.

20 cms

15 cms

15 cms → Fold

Card triangle points North.

Mark position of shadow hourly.

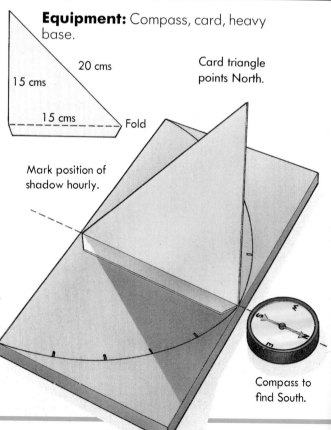

Compass to find South.

Meanwhile, the lower part of the Earth (the South) is farther from the Sun. The rays pass at a slanting angle through the atmosphere, where much of their energy is absorbed. It is winter in the South. As the Earth reaches the opposite side of its circle around the Sun, the seasons are reversed.

Draw a simple world map on a table-tennis ball. Carefully stick this on a pin, and shine a narrow-beam torch from the side. Twirl the ball slowly to show how day and night happen. Can you see why, on Earth, the Sun seems to travel across the sky?

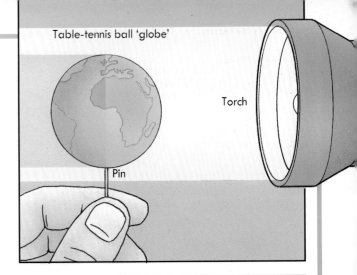

Table-tennis ball 'globe'

Torch

Pin

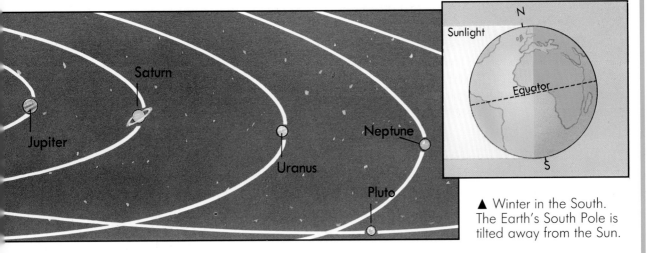

Saturn

Jupiter

Uranus

Neptune

Pluto

N

Sunlight

Equator

S

▲ Winter in the South. The Earth's South Pole is tilted away from the Sun.

▶ The Sun's light and heat rays are a powerful source of energy. Solar panels capture this energy and turn it into electricity. The car *Sunraycer* won a race across Australia, powered only by the Sun. Solar power will be important in the future, since it causes little pollution and the Sun will last for billions of years.

Where's the Hottest?

The highest temperature ever recorded was in Libya. The temperature was 58°C (136°F). And that was in the shade, which is the standard way to read the air temperature. In the sun it was hotter!

Measuring the Way the Wind Blows

When we say 'a north wind' we refer to the direction the wind blows from, not where it blows to. You can make a wind recorder (*right*) to measure the wind's direction.

Put a length of dowel through two cotton reels so that it spins easily. Glue one reel into the base of a shoebox, the other on the lid directly above, with a hole in the lid for the dowel. Tape a piece of paper to the lid, for the recording chart. Make a wind vane from a triangle of card, and fix a soft-lead pencil (6B) to its upright edge. Tape the middle of the vane to the dowel, so that as it spins the pencil draws a line on the recording chart. Place the wind recorder in an exposed place, steadied by stones in the shoebox. Draw a North–South line on the recording chart. As the wind changes direction, the pencil traces a line on the chart. The thickest part of the line shows where the wind has been blowing from for most of the time.

Equipment: Shoebox, two cotton reels, about 35 centimetres (14 inches) of dowel to fit in the reels, compass, 6B pencil, paper, glue, triangle of strong card, sticky tape.

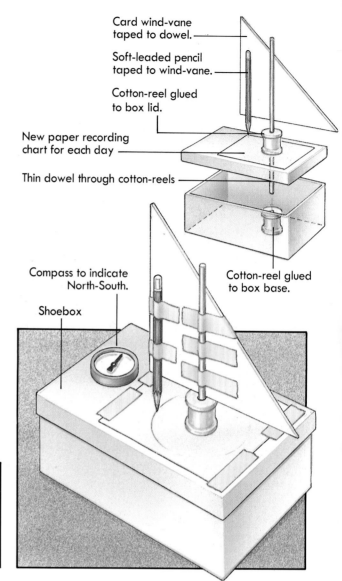

Card wind-vane taped to dowel.

Soft-leaded pencil taped to wind-vane.

Cotton-reel glued to box lid.

New paper recording chart for each day

Thin dowel through cotton-reels

Compass to indicate North-South.

Shoebox

Cotton-reel glued to box base.

The World's Winds

The Sun's heat energy warms different parts of the atmosphere by day and by night, and through the seasons. This keeps our weather on the move. Warm air is lighter than cold air and rises (*see page 5*). Cold air flows in to take its place. These movements create large-scale wind patterns or 'wind belts' around the world.

There are Polar Easterlies, Trades, and Prevailing Westerlies. Along the Equator is a region where winds seldom blow, the Doldrums.

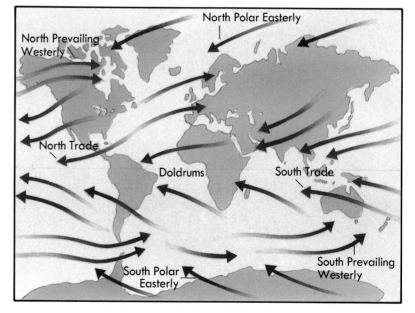

North Polar Easterly

North Prevailing Westerly

North Trade

Doldrums

South Trade

South Polar Easterly

South Prevailing Westerly

Water – Warm and Cold

Just as the Sun warms the atmosphere and creates winds, so it warms the surface of the oceans and helps to create water currents. You can demonstrate that cold water is heavier, or more dense, than warm water in your own bathtub!

How it works: Cold water is denser, or heavier than warm water and sinks to the bottom.

Put a few drops of food colouring in a plastic bottle. Fill this with cold water and shake it to colour the water evenly. Screw on the top and place the bottle in the fridge for a few hours, so that the water becomes even colder. Half fill the bath with warm water. Place the plastic bottle on the bottom. Carefully unscrew the top so that the cold, coloured water seeps out slowly. Watch how this cold, dense water spreads out – but stays near the bottom of the bath.

Equipment:

Plastic bottle of very cold water

Food colouring

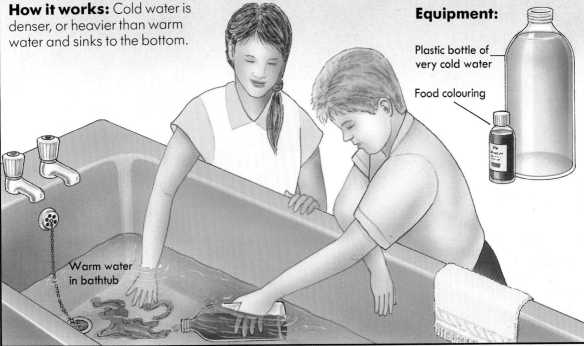

Warm water in bathtub

The World's Currents

The Sun's warmth and the winds, plus the spinning of the Earth, the tidal pull of the Moon and Sun combine to create oceanic water currents. The currents also change direction to flow around the great land masses.

These currents affect our weather, and they carry vast amounts of water. The West Wind Drift, which flows westwards around Antarctica, transports more than 200 times the amount of water carried by the Amazon.

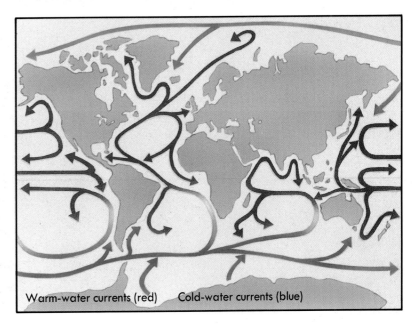

Warm-water currents (red)   Cold-water currents (blue)

Power from the Wind

We can capture the Sun's energy directly, as light and/or heat (*solar power, see page 9*). We can also capture it indirectly from the weather, by harnessing the power of the winds it creates. Like solar power, wind power produces little pollution, and it will be available as long as the Sun itself lasts.

Some people say that rows of huge windmills are a form of 'visual pollution'.

To make a windmill carefully cut four vanes in a star shape from stiff card, as shown below. Fold back a strip along one edge, on the same side, of each vane. Fix the star to a piece of dowel or cane, with a drawing pin through its centre, so that it is free to turn. Hold the windmill facing into a good stiff breeze, and it should spin rapidly. What happens if you fold the strips on each vane forwards instead of backwards?

▲▼ Windmills have been used for centuries (*above*), to grind wheat into flour, pump water and do other tasks. The modern version (*below*) converts wind power into electricity.

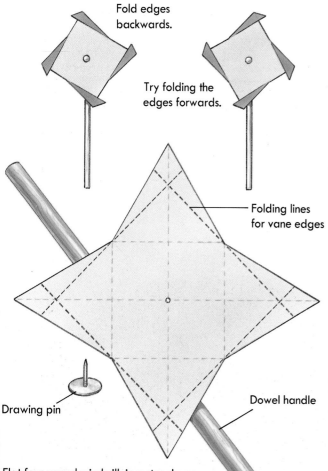

Fold edges backwards.

Try folding the edges forwards.

Folding lines for vane edges

Drawing pin

Dowel handle

Flat four-vaned windmill, in a star shape

Put a Sock in the Wind!

Windsocks are used at airports, sea ports and other exposed places such as mountain roads (*right*). The sock swivels away from the wind, which then blows into its open end or 'mouth'. The sock's tail points the way the wind is blowing. A stiff sock means a strong wind. If it flops loosely, the wind is only light. You can make a windsock using the instructions below.

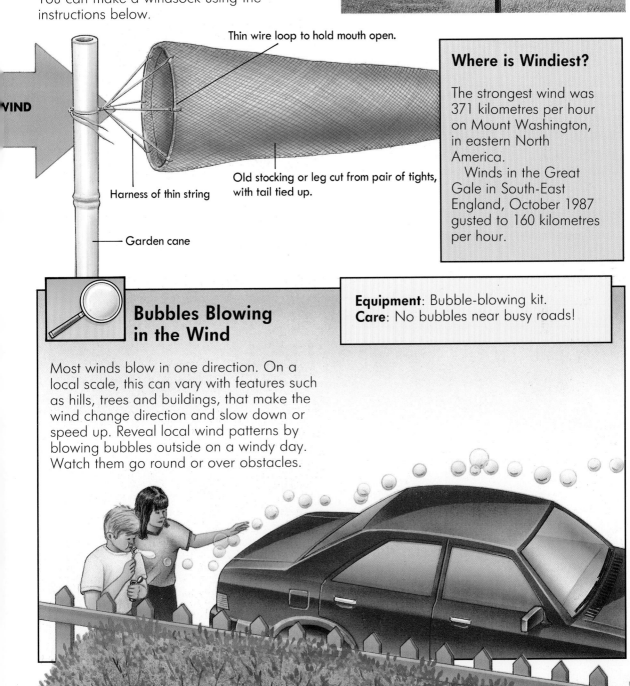

Thin wire loop to hold mouth open.

WIND

Harness of thin string

Old stocking or leg cut from pair of tights, with tail tied up.

Garden cane

Where is Windiest?

The strongest wind was 371 kilometres per hour on Mount Washington, in eastern North America.
   Winds in the Great Gale in South-East England, October 1987 gusted to 160 kilometres per hour.

Bubbles Blowing in the Wind

Equipment: Bubble-blowing kit.
Care: No bubbles near busy roads!

Most winds blow in one direction. On a local scale, this can vary with features such as hills, trees and buildings, that make the wind change direction and slow down or speed up. Reveal local wind patterns by blowing bubbles outside on a windy day. Watch them go round or over obstacles.

The Devastating Hurricane

A hurricane is formed when strong winds blow into an area of low air pressure (see page 30), and swirl violently in a circle. They develop over the warm tropical waters of the Atlantic Ocean, in the summer. Similar storms are called cyclones in the Indian Ocean, and typhoons in the Pacific.

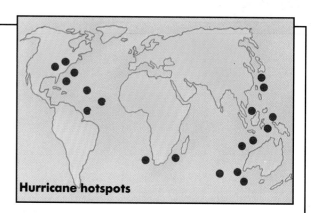

Hurricane hotspots

▲ Tropical storm hot-spots around the world. Where they hit the land, the strong winds do immense damage.

◀ Average wind speeds in a hurricane are at least 120 kilometres per hour (74 miles per hour). Yet in the 'eye' at the centre, there is hardly any wind at all.

▼ A satellite photograph of a hurricane over the Gulf of Mexico. The dashed lines show the coast. A computer has colour-coded the scene, with the strongest winds in red.

Hurricane

How Fast is the Wind Blowing?

With the help of an adult, you can make an **anemometer** to measure how fast the wind blows, as shown here.

Bend a loop at the end of a length of stiff wire. File the other end flat. Tape the loop to the bottom of a shoebox. Put stones in the box to steady it, and place the lid on, making a hole for the wire. Tape two thin pieces of wood into a cross. Push four paper cups onto the ends of the wood, facing in a circle. Securely fix the centre of the cross to the end (top) of an empty ballpoint pen tube with a

drawing pin and sticky tape. Push a pin through the tiny hole in the side of the tube, and place it on the wire upright, so that it pivots easily on the pin. Now take the anemometer to a windy place outside, on a table. (*Continued below.*)

Drawing pin

Pin in ventilation hole on side of pen case

Wooden cross pieces taped and pinned to pen tube.

Hole in shoebox lid

Empty ballpoint pen tube

Wire upright

Shoebox

Coathanger or similar wire, looped at bottom.

Loop taped into shoebox

Cotton thread

Modelling-clay weight

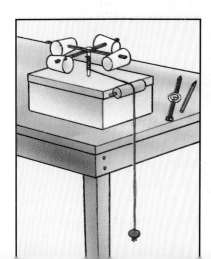

(*Continued from above.*) Tie a length of cotton to the pin in the side of the tube, leading it sideways over a roller (the centre of a kitchen roll). Let it hang down at the side of the table. Fix a small modelling clay weight at the end of the cotton, just touching the ground (*left*). Let the cups go, and they should swing round in the wind. Use a watch to

time how long the clay weight takes to rise from the ground to the edge of the table.

15

Moisture in the Air

The air in the atmosphere is hardly ever dry. It contains **water vapour**, which is the 'gas' form of water. Like other atmospheric gases, water vapour is invisible. But when the vapour turns to liquid (**condenses**) it forms small floating droplets of water, which we see as clouds, mist and fog. When the droplets become too big, they come down as rain.

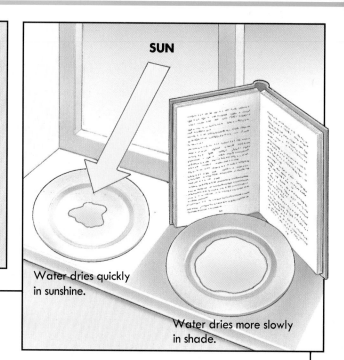

SUN

Water dries quickly in sunshine.

Water dries more slowly in shade.

'Disappearing' Water!

After a rainstorm, there are puddles everywhere. But when the Sun comes out, they soon disappear. Where does the water go? The Sun's warmth turns the liquid water into invisible water vapour, by **evaporation**. (Evaporation is the reverse of condensation.) The water 'dries up'.

Changing liquid water into vaporized water requires energy, usually in the form of heat. When our bodies get very hot, after much exercise, sweat droplets form on our skin. As the water in the droplets evaporates, it draws heat from the body and so we cool down.

You can show that the Sun's heat evaporates water by a simple experiment (*above*). Put two identical saucers on a sunny windowsill, and half-fill each with cold water. Put a 'sunshade' over one, such as a propped-up book.

How it works: Shielded from the Sun's rays, the water in the saucer dries less quickly than the water in full sunshine.

Equipment: Two saucers, water

Evaporating sweat from the skin cools the body when we are too hot.

Where's Foggiest?

Fog and mist are tiny water droplets floating in the air, like clouds at ground level. In a true fog, it is impossible to see clearly for more than 1000 metres (just over 1000 yards). On the Grand Banks, off Canada's Newfoundland, it is sometimes foggy for weeks on end. Here, there are true fogs for an average of one day in three each year.

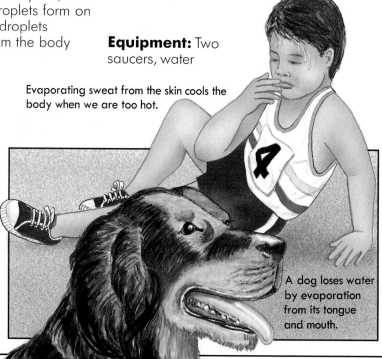

A dog loses water by evaporation from its tongue and mouth.

Humidity – Wet or Dry?

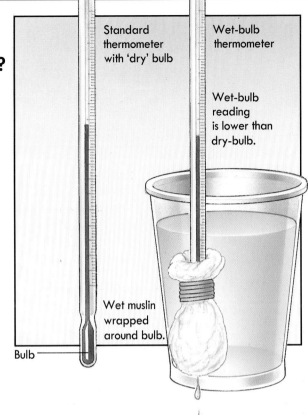

Standard thermometer with 'dry' bulb

Wet-bulb thermometer

Wet-bulb reading is lower than dry-bulb.

Wet muslin wrapped around bulb.

Bulb

The amount of water vapour in the air is called the humidity. When the humidity is low, sweat evaporates quickly from the body, and our skin feels dry. In high humidity, sweat cannot evaporate easily since the air already carries much water vapour. We say the weather is 'muggy' or 'sticky'.

Humidity level is measured by a psychrometer. This is made from two thermometers: a standard dry-bulb one, and one with wet muslin wrapped around it. Water evaporates from the wet bulb, and so this one registers a lower temperature. The greater the difference between the two readings, the lower the humidity.

▶ A home-made psychrometer needs two thermometers. The wet bulb must be kept very damp all the time for an accurate reading.

Handy Hints for Desert Survival!

Water is continuously evaporating into the air from many places on the Earth's surface, including seas, lakes, rivers, damp soil, wet roofs and roads, and plants and animals. This can be trapped as liquid water by a moisture trap, using the temperature change between day and night.

For people lost in the desert, this small drink could mean the difference between life and death. You do not have to be stranded in the desert, your own garden or park will do, provided you are allowed to dig a hole!

The Moisture Trap

Dig a conical hole and put in it a plastic beaker. In late afternoon, spread over it a plastic sheet, anchor it with large stones and place smaller pebbles in the centre (right). Cool air holds less water vapour than warm air. As the temperature falls at night, water vapour in the air and from the soil condenses on the plastic sheet and drips into the beaker.

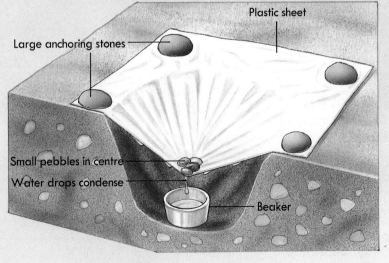

Plastic sheet

Large anchoring stones

Small pebbles in centre

Water drops condense

Beaker

Clouding the View

One of the most obvious features of our weather are the clouds floating across the sky. They are made of billions of water droplets formed from condensed water vapour, or of ice crystals made from frozen water droplets.

There are several main types of cloud, according to their shape and their height above the Earth's surface. For example, cirrus clouds are thin, wispy 'streams' at heights of over 10 kilometres (more than 6 miles). Cumulus clouds have flat bases and billowing, cotton-wool tops. Experts can predict the weather from the cloud types and the speed at which they move, blown by the wind. Cumulus may bring showers, while nimbostratus means long periods of rain.

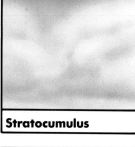
Cirrus

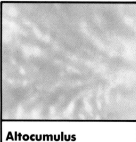
Stratocumulus

Cumulus

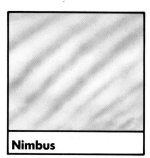
Altocumulus

Stratus

Nimbus

▲ 'Smog' is a combination of smoke and fog. It forms where air is polluted with vehicle exhaust fumes. There is a complicated chemical reaction between the fumes and the air, in the presence of sunlight. This smog-bound city is Santiago, in Chile. Smog can be prevented if cars become cleaner.

► Towering cumulonimbus are often called 'storm clouds'. They tend to bring lightning, thunder and heavy rain (see page 24). The dark base is only about 1 kilometre ($\frac{1}{2}$ mile) above the ground. The anvil-shaped spreading top may be over 6 kilometres (4 miles) high.

Cumulonimbus

Clouds in the Bathroom?

Run a warm bath in a cold bathroom and the air soon turns steamy and 'cloudy'. The 'steam' is a mixture of water vapour and tiny water droplets, like the ones that form clouds. It floats up in air which rises because it has been warmed by the hot water in the bathtub. Water vapour condenses on cold surfaces like the windows. These are like dewdrops, which condense from air onto the ground, when a cold night follows a warm day.

See 'Invisible' Dust!

Air is hardly ever perfectly clean. Tiny particles of dust float on the slightest wind. This is important, because each water droplet or ice crystal, in a cloud or fog, needs a tiny particle around which it can form and grow. It may be a piece of solid matter from dust or smoke, or salt from seaspray, or even chemicals from vehicle exhausts and factory fumes. You can see the 'invisible' dust in air by almost closing the curtains on a very sunny day.

How it works: Tiny pieces of dust glint in the narrow shaft of sunlight.

Particles of dust reflect sunlight.

The Water Cycle

The Earth always has about the same amount of water. This water is always on the move, in a never-ending cycle. The water cycle produces the most noticeable parts of our weather – clouds, fog, rain and snow.

Water vapour in the atmosphere condenses to form clouds and fog. Water falls to the surface as rain, and also frozen as hail and snow (see page 22). This 'fallen water' travels around on the surface. It filters through the soil, and runs in streams and rivers to the sea. Meanwhile, water is passing from the surface back into the air, as it evaporates to form water vapour. This 'risen water' also travels around in the atmosphere, carried as clouds and invisible water vapour blown by the wind.

▶ Water changes from vapour, to liquid, to solid and back again. The entire cycle is driven by heat energy from the Sun.

How Much Rain Have We Had?

You can record rainfall by making a simple rain gauge. Choose an open area such as a lawn, which is not shielded from the rain.

Bury a large jar with its neck at ground level. Carefully cut a small hole in the centre of a square sheet of stiff plastic (like the plastic packaging around toys). Choose a plastic funnel with the same diameter as the jar, cutting its top down if necessary. Jam its spout into the hole and put the sheet over the jar (right).

Each day, lift out the jar and measure the depth of rain water inside. This is how much rain has fallen since the last reading. Always tip away the water before replacing the jar!

Where is Wettest?

Rainfall is measured in millimetres (or inches) per year. The world's wettest place is Tutunendo, in Colombia, South America. Its average is 11,770 mm (463 inches) of rain each year! The average rainfall in London, England, is a mere 585 mm (24 inches)!

Equipment

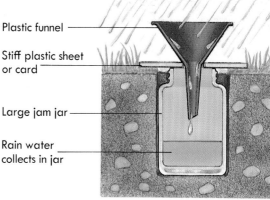

Plastic funnel

Stiff plastic sheet or card

Large jam jar

Rain water collects in jar

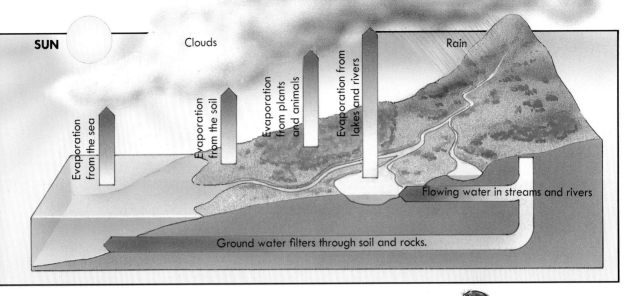

SUN

Clouds

Rain

Evaporation from the sea

Evaporation from the soil

Evaporation from plants and animals

Evaporation from lakes and rivers

Flowing water in streams and rivers

Ground water filters through soil and rocks.

From Raindrops to Dry Puddles

Here are two simple experiments to study rain. Find an area where a puddle always forms after rain, such as on paving stones or tarmac. When the rain stops, draw a line around the puddle's edge with a piece of chalk. Then draw another line each hour afterwards, to measure how fast the puddle dries out (*right*). Try the experiment in different kinds of weather. You can probably guess that the puddle will dry faster if the Sun shines. But what about wind? Does the puddle disappear faster on a calm day or a windy one?

You can also compare the number and size of raindrops. Carefully cut a large sheet of plain, absorbent paper, such as the

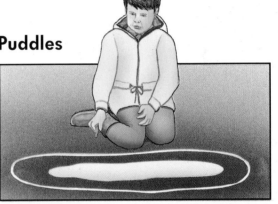

Chalk line marks edge of puddle 1 hour ago.

back of a spare length of wallpaper. Put the paper out in light drizzle for a certain time, such as five seconds. Quickly draw around the wet spots caused by the raindrops (*below*). Compare the result with the spots from a heavy shower.

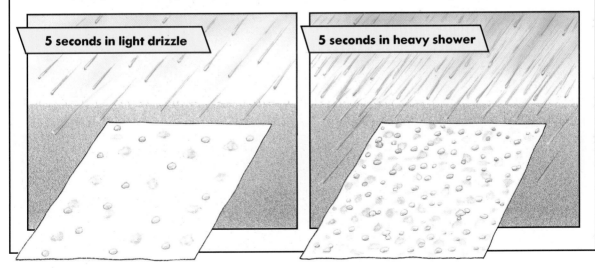

5 seconds in light drizzle

5 seconds in heavy shower

Rain, Hail and Snow

Water moves from the atmosphere to the Earth's surface in many forms, including rain, hail, snow, frost and dew. Sometimes the water goes straight back to the atmosphere. For example, a light snowfall may melt as soon as the Sun comes out, and the water evaporates back in the air. Or snow might fall in a very cold place, such as Antarctica, and be covered by more snow. Over time it is compressed into ice, and stays there for thousands of years. Both these journeys are part of the water cycle.

Raindrops usually form as ice crystals in a cloud, but they melt as they fall. Snowflakes form in the same way, but stay frozen if the air temperature is at or below freezing point (0°C, 32°F). Hailstones are raindrops that move back up into the cloud on rising air currents, and freeze into solid balls of ice.

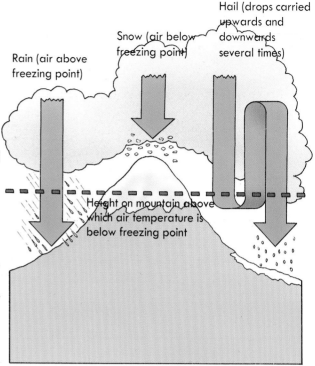

Rain (air above freezing point)

Snow (air below freezing point)

Hail (drops carried upwards and downwards several times)

Height on mountain above which air temperature is below freezing point

Rain

Snow

Hail

Biggest Hailstones

Most hailstones are pea-sized, but occasionally are large. A huge hailstone fell on Kansas, USA, in 1970. It measured 19 centimetres (7 inches) across and weighed 750 grams (1·6 pounds). Bigger ones have fallen, but no one has measured them before they melted!

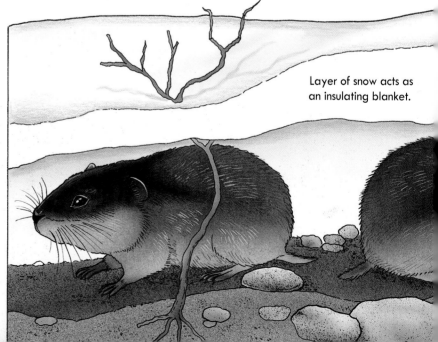

Layer of snow acts as an insulating blanket.

Be Jack Frost: Make a Pattern on a Plate!

Equipment: Petroleum jelly, glass plate.

At night, water vapour condenses from the air and normally forms dewdrops. If the surface temperature is below freezing, the water freezes into ice crystals, which we call frost.

To make a frost pattern smear a little make-up cream or petroleum jelly on your finger, and draw a design on a clean glass plate. Put the plate in a freezer next to a plastic beaker of warm water. The water vapour condenses and freezes on the clean parts of the plate, but not on the greasy parts. After an hour or two, your pattern is revealed!

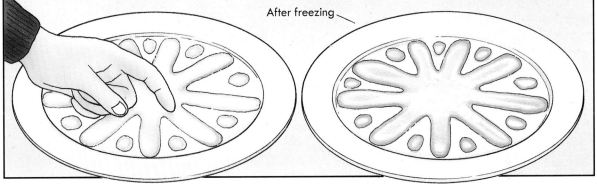

After freezing

Snug under the Snow

Snow may feel icy to us but in very cold places, such as the Arctic, a covering of snow acts like a blanket, that helps many creatures and plants to keep relatively warm. Above the snow, in the icy blasts of winter wind, the air temperature may fall to minus 4°C (about minus 40°F) or even lower. But the layer of loose snow holds tiny pockets of trapped air, just like a feather duvet. Air is a good insulator. Under their blanket of snow, creatures like lemmings and voles dig tunnels and continue to feed through the coldest weather. The temperature in the tunnels is only just below freezing – but that is much warmer than above the snow!

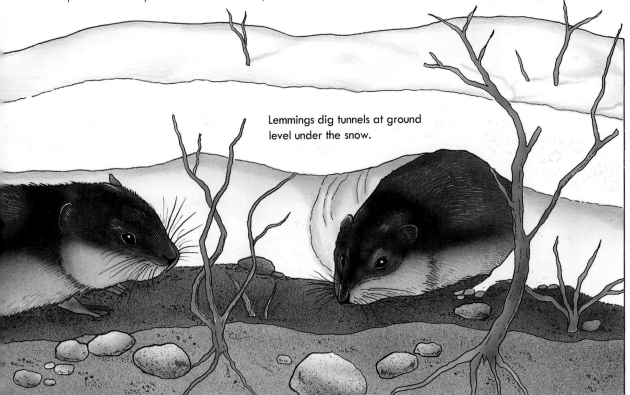

Lemmings dig tunnels at ground level under the snow.

Light and Sound

The weather can veer from one extreme to another in minutes. In a thunderstorm, deafening claps of thunder shake the ground and bolts of lightning split the dark sky. This is weather at its most powerful and violent. Yet soon after, the thunderclouds roll away, the wind drops, the Sun comes out, and a rainbow arches across the sky.

 Make Your Own Lightning!

Equipment: A large iron or steel saucepan (not aluminium) with a plastic handle, a rubber glove, an iron or steel fork, and a waste-bin liner.

You can make a tiny, harmless version of a lightning flash at home. Tape a plastic sheet to a table top. Hold a large iron saucepan by its insulating handle, with a rubber glove on that hand, and rub the pan vigorously to and fro on the plastic sheet. This gives the pan an electrical charge (see *opposite*). Then, holding

▲ The cactus desert of Arizona, USA, is lit up by jagged bolts of lightning known as 'fork lightning'. If the flash is far away, or spread out through the clouds, it is 'sheet lightning'.

a fork firmly in the other hand, bring its prongs slowly near to the saucepan's rim. When the gap between pan and fork is small, a tiny spark should jump across. (It may help to darken the room by drawing the curtains, to see the spark more clearly.) It is as though the pan is the 'thundercloud', the fork is the 'lightning conductor' (see *opposite*), and you are the 'Earth's surface'.

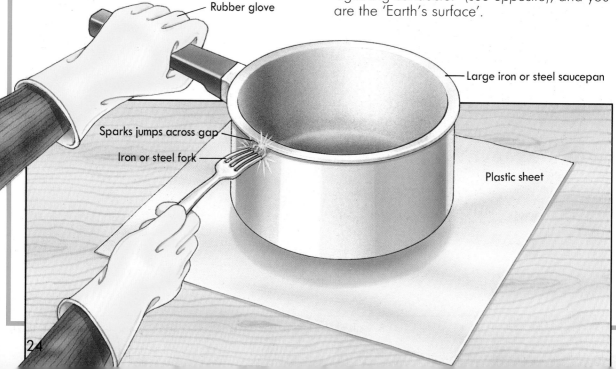

Rubber glove

Large iron or steel saucepan

Sparks jumps across gap

Iron or steel fork

Plastic sheet

How Far Away is Thunder?

In a thundercloud, small ice crystals, with positive electrical charges, float up near the top of the cloud. Larger ones, with negative charges, stay near the bottom. This separation of electrical charges is very unstable, and lightning is the way the charges are equalized again. The first part of the flash, the 'lead stroke', carries negative electricity down towards the ground. It is met by the 'return stroke' bringing positive charges up from the ground. The intensely hot lightning bolt heats the air around it, which suddenly expands, making the noise of thunder.

▶ Lightning and thunder are created together, but light travels faster than sound. Count the seconds between flash and clap, divide by 3. This is the storm's distance in kilometres.

Lightning Conductors

Lightning flashes do not always reach the ground. If they do, they head for tall objects sticking up from the surface, such as big trees or buildings. If lightning strikes a tree it may burst into flames. Lightning conductors prevent damage to tall buildings. These large strips of metal run between the topmost point and the ground. They give the lightning's energy a harmless route into the Earth.

▲ A jumbo-jet in storm clouds is lit by nearby lightning flashes. If lightning should strike, it spreads harmlessly over the aircraft, although it may disturb the flight instruments.

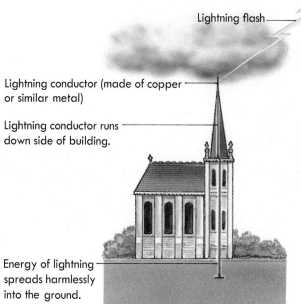

Lightning flash

Lightning conductor (made of copper or similar metal)

Lightning conductor runs down side of building.

Energy of lightning spreads harmlessly into the ground.

All the Colours of . . .

A rainbow is one of the most surprising, beautiful yet fleeting parts of the weather. It is caused by the Sun shining on raindrops. Each drop of water acts as a tiny prism (*see opposite*) and splits the almost-white sunlight into its separate colours (*see below*). On a bright sunny day, you can make your own small rainbow with a hosepipe. Turn on the water for a powerful flow. Place your thumb over the end of the pipe to scatter the water into thousands of tiny drops.

How it works: As the drops fall through the air, they act like rain and make a rainbow.

▶To see the rainbow, you must stand with your back to the Sun. The 'rain-bow' is in fact a 'rain-circle'. You can only see part of it from the ground. People in an aeroplane can see the whole circle.

ROYGBIV

Sunlight is a mixture of different colours of light, which the rainbow shows as separate. The main seven colours are always in the same order. Red is on the outside of the arc, then Orange, Yellow, Green, Blue, Indigo, and Violet inside. Remember this by the historical saying: 'Richard Of York Gained Battles In Vain.'

The Heat Haze

On a hot day you might see a 'heat haze'. The Sun heats up the ground more quickly than the air. The hot ground warms the air just above it, which then rises, carrying dust and other small particles. The rising air and dust interfere with light waves, bending them as they pass through, to produce the shimmering effect. A dark road is a good place to look, since the dull tarmac surface heats up well (*see page 7*).

. . . The Rainbow!

Equipment: White card, mirror, bowl.

A **prism** is a transparent object with angled sides, that bends the different colours in white light by different amounts. You can split sunlight to form a 'long flat rainbow' by making a 'long flat raindrop'.

Choose an open window in direct sunlight. Almost fill a bowl with clean water. Prop a piece of white card upright, next to the bowl. Hold a mirror in the water (*right*).

How it works: The curved water surface, where the water meets the glass, makes a prism that separates the colours in sunlight.

▼ The bright Sun can, in hot places, produce heat hazes and even mirages. In a mirage, light rays from the sky reflect off the layer of very hot air near the ground, and then up into your eyes. It is like looking into a mirror and seeing a reflection of the sky. Because the image is blue and wavy with heat haze, it looks like water.

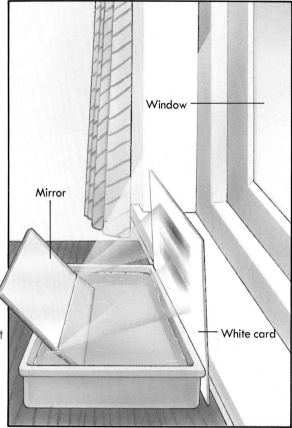

Window

Mirror

White card

Weather Forecasts

Weather affects us all. On a sunny day, we can go outside. If it is raining, we'll probably stay indoors. Farmers plant their crops when the soil is moist, and harvest them when the weather is dry. If we know what the weather is likely to be we can make better plans. A whole branch of science, **meteorology**, is devoted to the study of weather.

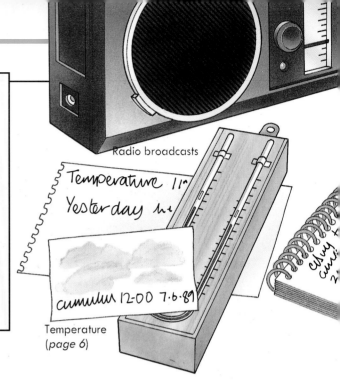

Radio broadcasts

Temperature
(*page 6*)

Your Own Weather Station

The various projects in this book show you how to build your own weather-measuring instruments and make weather records. On the right, you can see how to make a wind-strength recorder. It measures wind speed and direction at different heights above the ground (*see also page 15*). You can combine all your results in a Weather Notebook, along with information from the newspapers, radio and television. Include atmospheric pressure readings (*see page 30*) from a **barometer**. Look for patterns in the weather. For example, does a sudden fall in temperature and an increase in wind speed mean rain is more likely?

Gathering the Information

Weather experts, or meteorologists, collect information from many sources, as shown here. They also obtain measurements from other countries, as part of the worldwide weather-recording network. The recordings from each place must be made in the same way, so that they can be compared and combined accurately.

The methods and measurements are agreed by the World Meteorological Organization (WMO). For example, wind speed varies with height. So the WMO has set a standard height of 10 metres (33 feet) above the ground, for recording winds. Much of the information is nowadays fed into powerful computers, which can look for patterns in the weather.

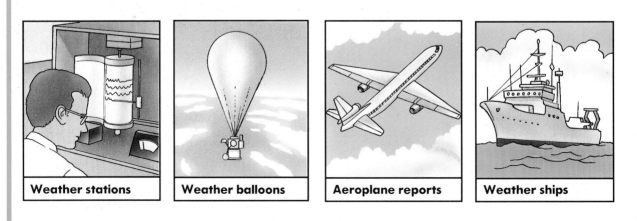

Weather stations   **Weather balloons**   **Aeroplane reports**   **Weather ships**

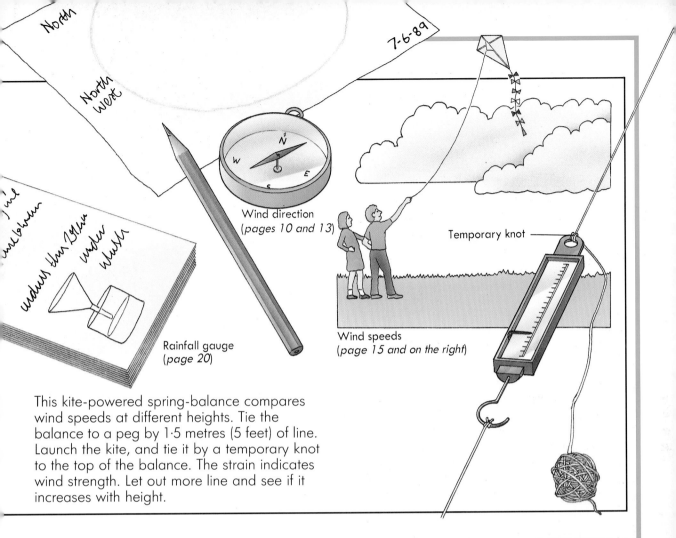

Wind direction
(*pages 10 and 13*)

Temporary knot

Wind speeds
(*page 15 and on the right*)

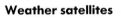
Rainfall gauge
(*page 20*)

This kite-powered spring-balance compares wind speeds at different heights. Tie the balance to a peg by 1·5 metres (5 feet) of line. Launch the kite, and tie it by a temporary knot to the top of the balance. The strain indicates wind strength. Let out more line and see if it increases with height.

▶ The control centre of a large meteorological centre is packed with computers, display screens and weather maps. Accurate forecasting of a big storm could save lives.

▶ A network of weather satellites, such as METEOSAT, send information down to ground stations.

Weather satellites

Weather aircraft

The Weather Map

Every day, the experts make weather forecasts that are given in the newspapers and on radio and television. Some people, like farmers and pilots listen to them regularly and are familiar with the special weather-words such as '**front**' and '**low**'.

One of the clearest ways of showing what the weather is doing is to draw a weather map. But what do all the lines, squiggles, numbers and arrows mean? Some of the main ones are described below. As you become more familiar with the words and symbols you can use your own weather observations to predict changes in the weather.

High pressure

The atmospheric air pressure (*see page 4*) varies with time, and from place to place. If it is higher than normal, this is called an area of high pressure or 'high'.

Low pressure

Places with lower than average atmospheric pressure are 'lows'. Pressure is measured in millibars (mbs). Standard atmospheric pressure at sea level is 1,013 mbs.

Isobar

On a map, contour lines join places of equal height above sea level. The lines (isobars) on the weather map join areas of equal atmospheric pressure.

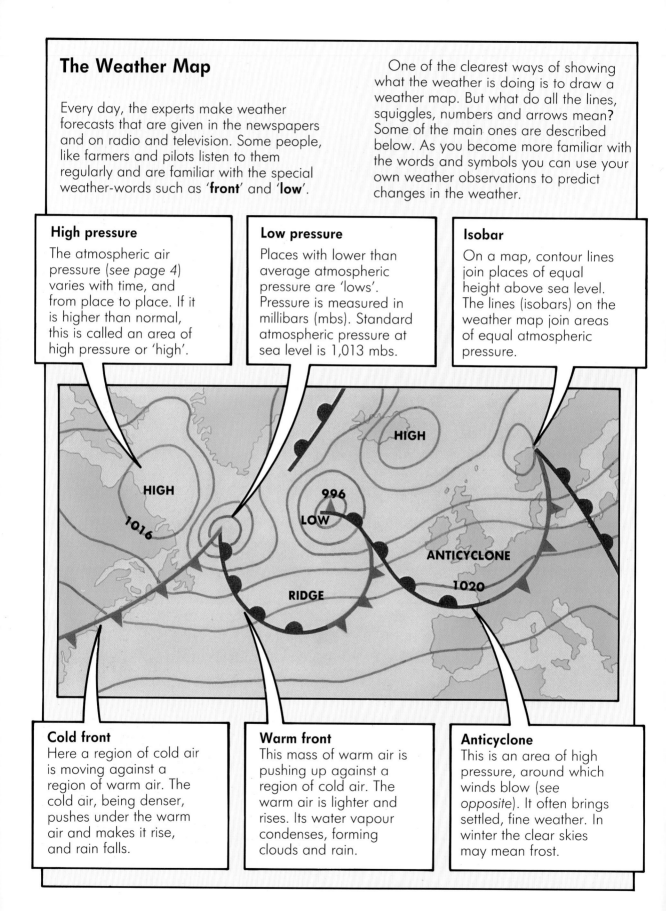

Cold front

Here a region of cold air is moving against a region of warm air. The cold air, being denser, pushes under the warm air and makes it rise, and rain falls.

Warm front

This mass of warm air is pushing up against a region of cold air. The warm air is lighter and rises. Its water vapour condenses, forming clouds and rain.

Anticyclone

This is an area of high pressure, around which winds blow (*see opposite*). It often brings settled, fine weather. In winter the clear skies may mean frost.

The High Pressure System

'Highs' or anticyclones take up vast areas of the Earth's atmosphere and affect the weather across whole continents. The 'high' is a region of high atmospheric pressure in which cool air sinks to the ground and then spreads out in the form of circling winds. The whole system may be thousands of kilometres across and 10 kilometres (over 6 miles) in height.

In the Northern Hemisphere (the northern half of the world, above the Equator) the winds blow in a clockwise direction. In the Southern Hemisphere, they blow anti-clockwise. This is a result of the forces generated by the spinning Earth, in what is called the Coriolis Effect.

▶ The sinking air in the centre of a 'high' usually means clear skies, sunshine and generally fine weather. This diagram shows a high pressure system in the Northern Hemisphere, where the winds spiral outwards in a clockwise direction.

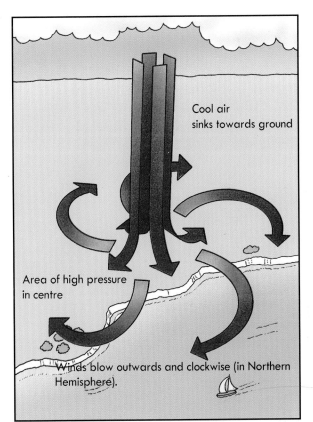

Cool air sinks towards ground

Area of high pressure in centre

Winds blow outwards and clockwise (in Northern Hemisphere).

The Low Pressure System

The 'low', also called a 'depression' or cyclone, is almost the reverse of the 'high'. Winds spiral inwards, in an anti-clockwise direction in the Northern Hemisphere, and clockwise in the Southern Hemisphere. The air in the centre rises, cooling as it does so. Cyclones in tropical areas may develop into hurricanes. Outside the tropics, they usually mean unsettled, wet, windy weather.

A typical 'low' is 2000 kilometres (1250 miles) across and up to 12 kilometres (7·5 miles) in height. Cyclones tend to move and change faster than anticyclones. They are born, then grow and mature, and finally fade away and die, in some cases within a few days.

▶ As air rises in a cyclone, it cools in the upper atmosphere to form clouds, and often rain. Western Europe, and especially the British Isles, are often affected by cyclones moving eastwards from the Atlantic Ocean, bringing strong winds and wet, blustery weather.

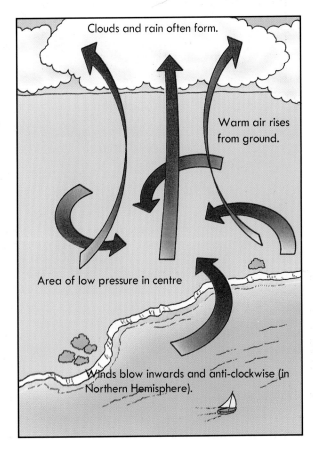

Clouds and rain often form.

Warm air rises from ground.

Area of low pressure in centre

Winds blow inwards and anti-clockwise (in Northern Hemisphere).

Weather Power

Every day, the land is under attack from the weather. Rocks are cracked by the Sun and by ice. Rain washes away loose soil. Rivers and glaciers rub great channels deep into the surface. The wind whips up waves that crash against the shoreline. These processes, known together as **weathering**, continually re-shape the landscape.

Make Your Own River!

Rivers are surface grooves along which water flows downhill. You can show how running water has the power to wear away, or erode, its banks. Place a layer of damp sand or soil on a large board, making a few 'hills' and 'valleys' in the landscape. Prop up one end of the board to make a shallow slope. Very slowly, trickle water from a jug onto the middle of the upper side. The water soon finds the quickest path down the slope. As it wears away a main channel, it carries away particles of sand or soil. This is erosion in action. (It is also why you should do this project outside!)

Equipment: Sand, board, water.

Trickle of water from jug

Water cuts away a 'cliff' on the outside of each bend.

A New Course

Over hundreds and thousands of years, huge land movements buckle and tilt the Earth's surface. Copy this by tilting the board slightly, to see how your 'river' finds a new course.

Board

Old river course before tilting

Sand or soil landscape

River

Sculpted in Stone

Over thousands of years, the forces of the weather can reduce the hardest of stone to dust. But the Earth's surface is made of many different rocks, some tougher than others. The softer rocks are worn away faster, leaving the hard ones. In the USA's Monument Valley, Arizona, hot sunshine and sand-blasting winds have rubbed away the softer rock to reveal harder 'stumps' of stone. To the west, the Colorado River (*left*) has cut the gigantic Grand Canyon deep into the Earth.

The Power of Ice

Water, like air, becomes more dense and contracts as it cools (*see page 5*). But when its temperature goes below 4°C (about 39°F), it begins to expand again and get bigger. As the water freezes into ice it continues to expand – and almost nothing can stop it.

Ice that forms in plumbing pipes may split them open. When the temperature rises and a thaw sets in, the ice melts, and the water floods out! This is why, in cold weather, it is important to wrap (lag) water pipes and protect them from the freezing temperatures.

▼ Fill an empty plastic ice-cream or margarine container with water, right to the brim. Clip on the lid, and place it in a freezer or icebox. As the water freezes into ice, it expands and pushes off the lid.

After freezing, the lid is pushed off by ice power.

Fill container to brim with clean water.

Ice-cream or margarine container

33

Weather and Climate

Weather shapes the physical world of rocks and running water. It also affects the living world – the types of plants and animals in each area. However, the word 'weather' applies to conditions in a small area, such as a county or state, and over a short time, during days or weeks. The word **climate** is used for whole countries and continents, and during long time periods, from years to many centuries. The world can be divided into several 'climate zones' (*see page 37*). In the tropics around the Equator, the climate is warm all year round, and daylight is very nearly 12 hours each day. At the North and South Poles, it is bitterly cold, and there is continuous daylight for half the year and darkness for the other half.

Mountain Climate Zones

1 Permanent ice and snow on the summit.
2 Alpine scrub, with cold winters and short summers.
3 Montane forest, often damp from cloud and rain.
4 Tropical forests need both high temperature and rainfall.
5 Tropical grasslands form in warm but drier regions.

Climate zones going up a mountain are similar to those going 'up the world' from the tropics to the North Pole (*see page 37*). Mountain zones are narrower. Temperatures fall by 1°C for every 155 metres (1°F for every 280 feet) above sea level.

1 Mountain ibex

2 Hedgehog

3 Tiger

5 Elephant

4 Orang utan

Houses Against the Weather

Probably the most widespread animal in the world is the human. People can live almost anywhere, from the tropics to the poles, because they build dwellings that shield them from the weather. The dwellings differ from one region to another, depending on local conditions such as the temperature, rainfall and wind, and also the local building materials. In addition, history and tradition shape our houses.

In the pine forests of the cold, snowy north, there are plenty of trees available. A common design is the log cabin (*right*, *above*). Its thick walls keep wind and snow out, and keep heat in.

The Tuaregs of the Sahara build tents of thin poles and animal skins (*right*, *middle*). The wide roof gives good shade, and open doors allow a cooling breeze. A 'typical English cottage' (*right*, *bottom*) has a roof thatched from locally grown reeds, small windows, and timber-framed or stone walls. It is cool in summer and warm in winter.

Log cabin

Nomad tent

How a house's heat is lost

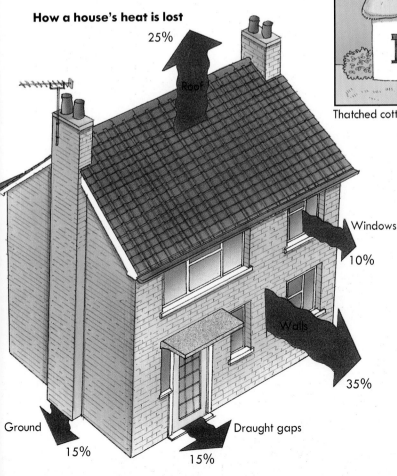

25%
Roof

Windows
10%

Walls

35%

Ground
15%

Draught gaps
15%

Thatched cottage

Today's Typical House

Many modern houses have been built to a standard square-box design. This makes a house easier and cheaper to build, but means that traditional dwellings with 'local character' are disappearing.

◀ In the past few years, we have realized that it is vital to save energy, especially from 'fossil fuels' such as coal, oil and gas. A typical house loses heat energy in many ways (*left*). We can cut down the waste by better building methods and materials, along with extra insulation.

Nature and the Weather

In natural wild places, plants and animals live in harmony with the weather and the seasons. With the warmth and moisture of spring, seeds begin to grow. Animals feed on the growing plants and begin to raise their young. In summer, the plants flower. Bees, birds and other creatures spread the flower pollen, helping to form seeds. In autumn the seeds and fruits ripen, while animals feed well and make stores for the winter. In winter many plants and animals go to 'sleep' until spring.

Gardeners must look after plants, weeding and watering, protecting them from animals, and perhaps raising them in a greenhouse. Left on their own, these 'unnatural' plants usually die, and the natural plants and animals take over.

Seaweed

Fir cone

Many plants use the weather, and especially the wind, to spread their seeds. Dandelion and thistle 'parachutes' float on the slightest breeze. Ash seeds, or 'keys', twirl away from the tall parent tree on their 'wings'. The wind shakes the seeds from ripe poppy capsules. As lupin pods dry out they suddenly snap open and fling their seeds away. A piece of seaweed absorbs moisture from humid air and becomes flexible and rubbery rather than stiff and dry. Fir cones open their scales in dry weather, to release the seeds within.

Dandelion seeds

Thistle seeds

Lupin seeds

Ash seeds

Weather Folklore

Many local sayings and legends are based on the weather. In Britain, 15 July is St Swithin's Day. It is said that if it rains on this day, it will rain for 40 days. Statistics show that the myth is not really true. In the USA, 2 February is Groundhog Day. It is said that the groundhog wakes up from winter sleep and looks outside its burrow. If it sees its own shadow, the weather is fine – but cold, so the groundhog goes back to sleep for six more weeks.

Poppy seeds

Animals Around the World

Wild creatures of the world cannot live anywhere. A gorilla could not survive in the icy wastes of Antarctica. An Arctic hare would not live long in a tropical forest. Each kind of animal is suited only to a certain climate. The climate has direct effects on the animal itself, by its temperature, humidity, rainfall and winds. It also has effects on the surrounding animals and plants, which provide food and shelter for others, and which are all tied into the natural network of life.

The broad wildlife zones across the world are known as 'biomes', and they resemble the different zones as you travel up a mountain

(see page 34). However, some animals have been able to 'cheat' nature and spread to unsuitable areas – but only with our help. Farm animals such as sheep, cattle, goats and pigs are fed and housed by us, in places where they could not otherwise survive. Cats, dogs and other pets rely on us for food and shelter. More unwelcome guests like rats and mice survive almost anywhere that we do.

▼ The diagram below shows the main climate zones from the Equator to the North Pole, and examples of animals from each zone. There are similar zones towards the South Pole.

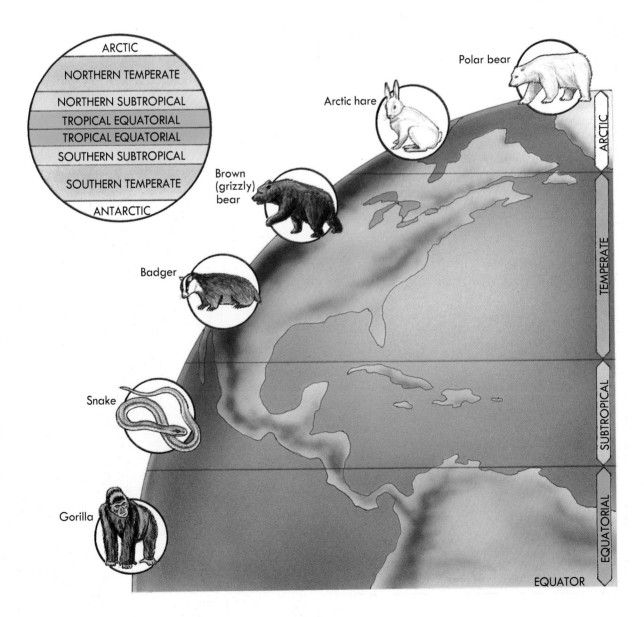

A Change in the Weather?

The Earth's climate has changed many times in the past. Subtropical forests have spread from the south into temperate areas. Millions of years later, ice sheets have spread from the north. Today, the great danger is that we are changing the climate. Can Earth survive?

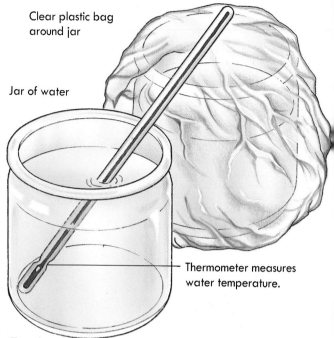

Clear plastic bag around jar

Jar of water

Thermometer measures water temperature.

 ## The Greenhouse Effect

In bright sunshine, the air inside a greenhouse becomes warm. The greenhouse glass lets in the Sun's light energy and some of its heat energy. Inside, part of this energy is 'reflected' and converted into a different type, which cannot pass back out through the glass so easily. The energy, in the form of heat, builds up inside the greenhouse.

You can show this with two identical glass jars, each containing cold water. Wrap one in a plastic bag (this is the greenhouse 'glass'). Leave them in the Sun for an hour. Then measure the temperature of the water in each jar (above). Which is warmer?

Equipment: Thermometer, glass jar, plastic bag.

The same thing is now happening to the Earth. Over the past few centuries, people have been burning fuels such as wood, coal, oil, gas and petrol, in ever-increasing amounts. The gases formed by the burning, such as carbon dioxide, are building up in the atmosphere. They act like greenhouse glass. The result: experts believe the Earth will heat up and undergo '**global warming**'.

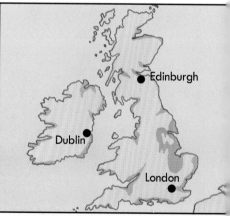

◀ ▲ Burning large areas of forest speeds the Greenhouse Effect. As the Earth warms, the oceans will expand and polar icecaps will melt. The rise in sea level could flood many major cities (*above*).

Acid Rain

The weather can transport pollution across seas and continents. Power stations (*right*), factory chimneys and vehicle exhausts pour all manner of chemicals into the atmosphere. They include sulphur dioxide and nitrous oxides. These react with substances already in the atmosphere, and with water, to form weak acids. The polluted clouds and air float for hundreds of kilometres on the wind.

Eventually the acidic moisture falls to Earth as rain – acid rain. The acids damage trees,

▲ Power stations are one of the main sources of fumes that make acid rain.

rivers and lakes, killing fish and other water creatures. They even eat away statues and the stonework of buildings.

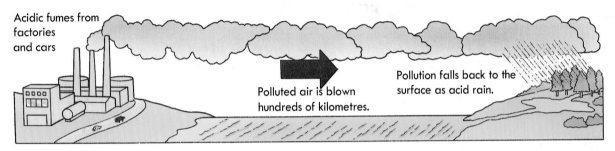

Acidic fumes from factories and cars

Polluted air is blown hundreds of kilometres.

Pollution falls back to the surface as acid rain.

The Ozone Hole, and How We Can All Help

Many of today's products could alter our climate in the future. Recently, experts discovered that certain chemicals in aerosols and fridge cooling fluids are entering the atmosphere and damaging the **ozone layer**. This layer of ozone gas, high in the atmosphere, filters out much of the

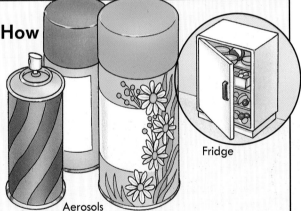

Fridge

Aerosols

Sun's harmful rays. If the layer becomes thinner or disappears, damaging rays would reach the surface. They could cause many problems, such as an increase in skin cancers.

Manufacturers are now making 'ozone-friendly' aerosols to help reduce the risks.

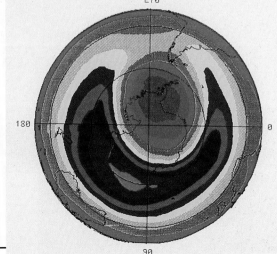

◄ This computer-coloured satellite photo shows the thinning of the ozone layer over Antarctica, in late 1988 The developing 'hole' is coloured in blue.

Index

Page numbers in *italics* refer to illustrations, or where illustrations and text occur on the same page.

Editor: Thomas Keegan
Designer: Ben White
Illustrators: Kuo Kang Chen
                Peter Bull
Consultant: Terry Cash

Cover Design: Pinpoint Design Company
Picture Research: Elaine Willis

Photographic Acknowledgements
The publishers would like to thank the following for kindly supplying photographs for this book:
Page 6 J.F.P. Galvin: 7 ZEFA; 9 Allsport/Simon Bruty; 12 ZEFA (top) Science Photo Library (bottom); 13 Frank Lane Picture Agency; 14 Science Photo Library; 18 ZEFA; 24 ZEFA; 25 ZEFA; 27 Science Photo Library; 29 Crown Copyright/Reproduced with the permission of the Controller of Her Majesty's Stationery Office; 32 The Hutchison Library; 38 South American Pictures; 39 ZEFA (top) Science Photo Library (bottom).

Kingfisher Books, Grisewood and Dempsey Ltd, Elsey House, 24–30 Great Titchfield Street, London W1P 7AD

First published in 1990 by Kingfisher Books
10 9 8 7 6 5
© Grisewood and Dempsey Ltd. 1990

All rights reserved. No part of this publication may be reproduced, stored in a retrieval system or transmitted by any means, electronic, mechanical, photocopying or otherwise, without the prior permission of the publisher.

BRITISH LIBRARY CATALOGUING IN PUBLICATION DATA

Parker, Steve, *1952—*
    Weather
    1. Weather
    I. Title II. Series
    551.5
    ISBN 0–86272–533 X

Phototypeset by Wyvern Typesetting Ltd, Bristol
Printed by: South China Printing Company H.K.